WRITING OUR LIVES
Volume II

A Southern Storytellers Anthology

Introducing

Chelsey Barton • Alexis Diane Finks
Phyllis Hodges • Jonelle Grace Lipscomb
Jean Hicks McIntosh • David Nickell
Monieca West • Yolanda Winston

© 2017 by Janis F. Kearney

All rights reserved. No part of this book may be reproduced or transmitted in any form or by any means, electronic or mechanical, including photocopying, recording or by any information storage and retrieval system, without permission in writing from Writing Our World Publishing, 2 Rosier Court, Little Rock, Arkansas 72211.

First Writing Our World Press Edition
Volume II 2017
Printed in the United States of America

Edited by Shelly S. Cantrell
Interior Design by Shelly S. Cantrell

Cover Design by
Kenosis Design Innovations

ISBN 978-098-480253-1

www.writingourworldpress.com

To the brave southern writers
who keep making our world better
by sharing their joys and pain.

CONTENTS

Foreword
Janis F. Kearney 6

Dreams . Resilience . Love
Chelsey Barton 15

Freedom
Alexis Diane Finks 27

School Days
Phyllis Hodges 35

Visiting Mother
Jonelle Grace Lipscomb 41

The House at the End of the World
Jean Hicks McIntosh 51

Washtubs and Empty Lots
David Nickell 59

Darling Daughter
Monieca West 65

Word of God in Motion
Yolanda Winston 74

FOREWORD

It happened in 2015. Ten brave writers came together in the first Writing our Lives Memoir Writing Workshop, seeking answers. They left, eight months later, with more questions but greater courage. Already writers inside, in their spirits, they left knowing that a writer's mission is to transport ourselves—our memories, our secrets, our joys and pains—from inside us to the blank sheet of paper.

Terrifying? Absolutely. But, whoever said transformation was an easy thing? Whether the transformation is from a ditch digger to a floor manager or a dreamer to a writer, change is a most difficult and scary task.

Yet, the brave writers of 2015 refused to give up, or give in. And in repayment for their courage, they discovered that transformation could be just as exhilarating as it is scary and difficult.

They learned that writers don't become great at the art simply because they've wanted it for so long or because their high school English teacher told them they should write. They learned that becoming an author or a published writer means turning yourself inside out for the art of storytelling. It means you fully accept your mission of sharing your life with others.

For the strange creatures that write, our stories and the sharing of our stories keep us alive. For many of us it is the reason for waking each morning, for putting one foot in front of another, and for going bravely into the world full of hope in tomorrow.

Presented here are stories from members of that courageous group of writers who dare share themselves with you. Some are short stories. Some are excerpts from longer manuscripts. All are memoirs, the southern writers' offering of their truth.

I'll begin with mine.

GOODBYE COLORED EDUCATION.
HELLO FREEDOM OF CHOICE

Excerpt from Cotton Fields of Dreams: A Memoir

by Janis F. Kearney

2017: The 60th anniversary of the most renowned integration effort in America, the Central High Integration Crisis of Little Rock. I offer this reminiscence of my hometown, Gould, Arkansas' own struggle with integration, which took place some ten years later. I am yet nostalgic for that pivotal moment in my life. There was something innately beautiful about our racially restrictive colored education and something terrifying about the new Freedom of Choice.

Gould's black schools mirrored so many others in Arkansas' Delta region—sparse population with no industry to speak of and endless acres of almost blinding white cotton fields. Though we never used the word and wasn't aware of its presence, the Jim Crow Laws were an incipient part of everything we experienced in the Arkansas Delta. Years later, though, we all agreed that for young, poor children there might have been an ironic blessing in that terrible law. In spite of our needs, black children in towns like Gould were blessed to have teachers and school administrators who believed their mission was to lay a foundation for our future. Both history and personal experiences made them understand the obstacles before us; and the majority of them worked hard to prepare us for the mountains and molehills that might obstruct our paths.

The school boards were made up of both good and not so good white citizens who were all, like us, victims of the times and their

FOREWORD

environment. Black children's' education was not a priority. The most that was expected of even our best and brightest were future careers in teaching, becoming a clerk or entry-level state government jobs.

Many black children—including the Kearney children—grew up believing our tomorrows could be something more than what we saw in front of us. Our parents and teachers with vision helped us see those possibilities. They took the sour lemons life gave them and made the best lemonade money could buy.

I attended Fields Elementary School, an all black school, from 1959 to 1965. When my teacher distributed textbooks, the first thing I did was peer inside the front cover. There on the dark lines were hand-written names, scrawled haphazardly. I knew they were the white students' names because my father had railed about the used books his and other black children received from the white school.

The worn, sometimes tattered books were one more symbol of our second-classed citizenship. When I was able to read well enough, I read the white children's names out loud, "Laura, Michael, Susan, Debbie, Sarah...." I tried imagining the white faces and how their lives differed from mine. I wondered if Laura or Susan had little brothers or sisters as I did. Did they fight? What did they talk about at night when they laid in bed; and did they all share beds, too?

I would imagine that the girl or boy had held this very book took it home and copied homework from its pages. I knew they would be given new books with shiny, unmarred covers and a new book smell. Their books would have blank lines inside, awaiting their own fresh scrawl. No Laura or Michael or Sarah owned the books before them.

FOREWORD

When desegregation finally forced its way into Gould in 1967, the white leaders offered black families the South's version of experimental school integration called "Freedom of Choice." Black parents, including mine, may have understood that they and their children were on trial; but that didn't stop them from hurriedly signing us up and shuttling us off to the domain of the white school system. They had dreams of their children acquiring a quality education, something that would take us further than becoming a teacher or a clerk.

The white children's names in the cover of our texts had haunted me all those years. Those last summer days before we entered the white school, I dreamed of finally meeting the Laura, Sarah or Michael I imagined years before. I wanted to match those names from the books with the faces to which they belonged. I found Michael by the second week of school. It took me longer to find Sarah. The second-hand books had afforded me a glimpse of these students while they knew nothing about me.

In spite of what I may have missed in quality during my years at the segregated black school, years later I realized the value of my early school years. I treasured the black teachers who cared for me and made a difference in my life. Those women and men not only identified with other students and me but also believed in our capabilities.

In many ways, black schools offered second-rate education. We were stuck with hand-me-down books, little funding for extra-curricular activities, plus sparse maintenance and repairs of our schools. Our education was secondhand, just like the clothing I wore most days. Both were previously used and tattered but still functional... still in good enough shape to serve a purpose. Great

FOREWORD

minds were nurtured and expanded in the midst of that second-hand education.

Most teachers who came to our schools came with a mission—to prove the world wrong about black children's inability to learn. They didn't come armed with preconceived notions about black children's worth or their abilities based on the color of their skin. Because they didn't have a long list of options in what schools they would work, they were primed to work against the tide—to transcend their physical environments to give us the best education they knew how.

Many of our teachers were not much older than the high school students they taught. They already felt the wind of change, however, and their efforts were spent preparing us for change. For black communities, our academic successes represented success for our race. Our teachers toiled in the often-bare schoolrooms to transform the rough diamonds we were into smooth, sparkling gems that would one day make the world sit up and take notice. They were nurturers of our young minds and spirits and the foundation upon which we began our lives.

~

All during the Pre-Civil Rights era, a quality education for black children was never a priority of Gould's all-white school board. In my twelve years at Gould's public schools, I was blessed to have many gifted teachers and only a handful of those who were teachers in name only. My first six years were at Fields—memorable years that would stay with me through the best and worst of times. My two years in the experimental freedom of choice program at the all-white Gould Public Schools left scars and created questions about what "quality" education truly meant.

FOREWORD

In 1967, after two years of Gould's integration practice, the school board agreed to the Federal Government's desegregation plan. The former all-black Fields High School took the name of the former all-white Gould High School. The former Gould High School became Gould Elementary. Like most southern towns, the black institutions lost a great deal in the process. In spite of the fact that less than ten percent of the 500-student population was white, neither of the formerly all-black institutions existed after September 1967.

My experiences at this new high school greatly differed from my earlier experiences at both Fields Elementary and Gould School. It was as if my younger sister Jo Ann and I were convinced our time at the white schools had magically transformed us in the eyes of our former classmates and schoolmates.

Suddenly teachers and students saw something more than the poor, ragged Kearney girls who had left the black school in 1965.

In the four years I remained at Gould High, my self-esteem soared. My popularity quadrupled, I was actively involved in extracurricular activities, and I served as Captain of the cheerleading squad for three years. Without the transformation, this would never have happened to Janis Kearney from Fields Elementary School. The real Janis Kearney was still there, though, watching the miraculous transformation with awe and some wariness.

Ninety percent of Gould's white parents, even those teaching at Gould High, attempted to stay one step ahead of the school desegregation law, by shuttling their children off to the new private academies popping up along Highway 65 and in other areas of the state. Some well-to- do parents, and others barely making ends meet, used their savings accounts and changed their addresses to assure their children continued learning in a segregated environment.

The late 1960s and early 1970s meant dramatic changes in everyday life for small Southern towns such as ours. The old comfortable relationships between whites who accepted their first-class citizenship and blacks who pretended to accept their second-class citizenship suddenly changed before our eyes. The court's desegregation laws meant we were suddenly equal in every way and the relationships would never be as comfortable again.

The country's well-intentioned integration effort took its toll on our small town. While black residents were valiantly trying to catch up with the rest of the world, white residents were valiantly trying to hang on to the past. The funding of their children's private educations ruined many of the rich, white families who mortgaged homes, sold off hundreds of acres of land, and traded their wealth and standing in the community for a trailer-house classroom that guaranteed no black faces.

Whether it was part of this tragic tumble or an incidental sidebar of the times, cotton was fast losing its luster and value in the South; and white students whose parents had gone broke educating them in segregated schools, were deciding in droves that education wasn't such a big deal after all. An amazingly small number went on to college after their private academy education.

FOREWORD

Janis F. Kearney is a writer, publisher, journalist, and writing instructor. She purchased the historic Arkansas State Press Newspaper from Civil Rights legend Daisy Gatson Bates in 1988. She was appointed as the first-ever Personal Diarist to a President in 1995, tasked with chronicling the presidency of William J. Clinton. In 2001, she was selected as a fellow at the W.E.B. DuBois Institute of African and African American Studies at Harvard University. In 2004, she was selected as a Humanities Fellow at Chicago's DePaul University, and in 2007, as a Visiting Humanities Scholar and Professor at Arkansas State University, Jonesboro. In 2003, Janis founded Writing our World Publishing. While she serves on numerous non-profit boards and committees, her most important work is serving as the Founding President of the Celebrate! Maya Project of Arkansas, which started in 2014 after the death of literary icon, Maya Angelou. The project seeks to increase the awareness of Maya Angelou's life and legacy throughout the state and to help youth in the Arkansas Delta realize their academic and artistic dreams through literary programs, scholarships, and awards.

DREAMS . RESILIENCE . LOVE
A Young Woman's Journey Through Life

by Chelsey Barton

Forrest City, Arkansas: a place I call home, a place surrounded by dirt roads in every direction. Cotton fields flank every side, and mosquitos wait to greet you day and night. Founded by Nathan Bedford Forrest, the general of the Confederate army in 1827, Forrest City is located directly off Interstate 40E as you head to Memphis, Tennessee from Little Rock, Arkansas. I like to call it The Heart of the Delta.

I remember growing up, riding in the back seat of the car, looking out the window at the mom and pop's shops, driving past churches on every corner and being greeted by Mrs. Robinson, who knew everyone and everything; but everyone knew everyone's business. That wasn't uncommon for a small, southern town in The Heart of the Delta. Little occupied our minds so we indulged in baseball at the park, going to local sporting events, hanging out at the skating rink, playing at the south side park, walking through Wal-Mart or enjoying time with friends and family.

When I was a child, my paternal grandparents lived in the county of Forrest City, St. Francis County. We visited them and enjoyed the farm animals—chasing baby chicklings, running away from aggressive geese and feeding the hogs. On bright and humid, summer mornings, I helped my grandparents till the ground in their garden to prepare for greens, peas, cabbage, watermelon and corn in the upcoming growing seasons.

Oh how I loathed corn.

After long mornings in the garden, I enjoyed sitting at the pond with my aunt and waiting for a big catfish or bass to take my bait. At night as the night critters came out, we sat outside on my grandpa's pickup truck watching the stars in the sky—dreaming of the known and unknown universe. On Sundays, we went to church with my grandparents. My grandfather made sure that everyone who stayed over night on Saturday went to the house of the Lord on Sunday mornings. To this day I do not know how my grandfather enforced that rule with my older cousin; but with me, I had got a whooping with the nearest peach tree switch if I wasn't up and ready for Sunday School at 9:30am sharp.

One Sunday during Black History Month, I reflected over the great and brave people who paved the way for future generations to create a change in human history that would transform the dynamics of the social economic system between race and creed. I thought to myself: What would I do to go down in history? How will I impact people's lives?

These great men and women inspired something in me. They lived for something far greater than themselves, far greater than their century. I wanted to do the same thing. Even then in my life, no more than shy of eight years old, in my heart I knew I could accomplish things far greater than my generation or myself. I just needed to figure out what my purpose was in this lifetime.

Growing up we didn't have much. It's funny because looking back I did not know how poor we actually were until I became an adult. My parents were young when they had me. I am the oldest of five children. They were eighteen when they got married and began having children. My father is the oldest son of seven children. My mother is the second to eldest daughter out of five children. My father grew up on a farm. His parents had him at an old age. I do not know much about his life. I only know of a few memories that his family members shared with me. I was told he liked to sing and he used to pretend he was a preacher. One day he built an altar and pretended to preach before a congregation. That is all that I know about my father. Looking back at his childhood photos, he seemed so gentle and mild- mannered.

My mother was born in Forrest City, Arkansas. Her mother was originally from Mississippi. Her grandmother was the daughter of one of the original owners of Simmons Bank. Her maternal grandparents lived in Moro, Arkansas. Her paternal grandmother lived in Forrest City, Arkansas. She always mentioned the hardships of her childhood and how her father was an abusive man; but that is it. She never went into greater detail about her life.

Even as an adult, I know very little about my parents.

My parents fought a lot. I don't recall many happy family memories of both parents in the home. Three of my siblings spent a lot of time living with our paternal grandparent. I stayed with my maternal grandparents. By the time I was nine, my parents decided to divorce. After the divorce, we experienced increase rejection from our parents. Being the oldest child, I stepped in to raise my siblings. I took on the responsibility of babysitting, cleaning, and cooking for them.

Confrontational meetings between my mother and me increased during my teenage years. She cursed at me, attempted to fight with me or would put me out of her house. By the time I was a junior in high school I became accustomed to our daily routine of hatred bouts. My boyfriend, at the time, asked me daily if I was put out of the house again. I never hit my mother or cursed her out because of the precious lesson my paternal grandfather instilled in me. He introduced me to God the Word of God.

I grew up reciting the Ten Commandments. I held the first commandment very close and dear to my heart. So, no matter how evil my mother acted or how badly I wanted to fight back to regain the confidence of my ego, I never hurt my mother. I stayed still. I did not curse at her because of the first commandment: honor thy mother and thy father. I lived by that no matter how foolish and weak I felt in walking away from her.

When I was 17, my mother officially put me out of her home. I honestly cannot say why she put me out. I just know she told me I could no longer live with her. I went to live with her older sister to finish out high school. I finished high school without any parental support. I decided that I wanted more out of life than what had been presented to me during my younger years. I wanted to go on vacation, own nice things and provide for my family. I always felt that my parents didn't love my siblings and me because they could not take care of us. They struggled financially. The feeling of being unloved went deeper than the monetary things; it stemmed from my parents' actions.

My parents chose to selfishly do things for themselves, instead of nurturing their children; but I must say, although my parents did not show love through actions, words, or their sacrifices, there was always someone strategically aligned in my life to show me love and nurture me in the way I needed at the specific time, so I could continue to move toward my dreams—even if I did not know how

I would achieve them. God placed people throughout my life to help me achieve major milestones such as earning a college degree. While in college, I sent money to my siblings to help pay for essentials. I encouraged them to graduate from high school, to go off to college and to become more than a stereotype. Statistically, we should have been pregnant, on drugs or in the streets. We overcame the stereotypes.

My life change drastically on October 17, 2013 when I became a widow after only two and half years of marriage. I know that might not seem like a long marriage. In reality it was not, but we had been in each other's lives for over a decade. My husband was the man of my dreams—literally.

He was my dream man.

Alvin Travis Barton (AJ) was born to Mr. and Mrs. Alvin and Lorita Barton in Memphis, Tennessee on December 3, 1984. Prior to AJ's birth, his parents suffered the loss of three babies at birth. As I listened to AJ's mother share her beautiful story of faith, I thought to myself that AJ was a miracle baby. People encouraged her quit trying to have a baby, but she knew deep in her heart that God would bless her with a baby. God did just that. He honored the cry, the belief in her heart, and He blessed her with a strong, healthy baby boy.

My husband was a very nice man. He was respectful and intelligent—full of wisdom and endless boundaries to where his mind could expand. He could talk to anyone about anything. He once told me that he knew a little about a lot of things so he could hold a conversation with anyone about any subject. He simply amazed me with his beautiful mind. When I told him that his mind was so beautiful to me and I was greatly attracted to it, he gave me his infamous smirk and kept talking.

Even with all of the beautiful attributes he possessed, my husband battled a war within: depression. Even he did not know what triggered this illness; however, he knew God strategically positioned him to be around people who loved him. I pointed out the relationships he had with his friends, the love he received from his family and that even in all of the suffering he had undergone God was always around.

God is love.

AJ's family loved him. They loved him dearly. So even when he felt empty inside, with pain and torment, God was always there through people. I looked at my husband—a man with endless boundaries of potential. He was a bright, beautiful young man inside and out. He never wished harm on anyone. He just wanted to live a fulfilling life.

On a cold, sunny morning in February 2011, I sat at my kitchen table talking to God about my then boyfriend. I opened my Bible to Psalm 91. I read that entire passage out loud to myself, and then I sat there looking out into the distance and I uttered these words: God I will live for you for real if you save this man (AJ). He has so much great potential. I know in your word you said you are a deliverer, you are a healer. God he is not living his full potential. God please heal him. I will stand in the gap for him I will serve you to save him. God heal him. Save his soul. Save his life. Restore onto him his mind. Help him to reach his full potential in life because as long as he suffer from this illness he will never really live the life you intended for him to live.

DREAMS . RESILIENCE . LOVE

I did not realize that during that moment, that prayer was a pivotal moment in my spiritual walk with God and the change I had witnessed in the healing and deliverance for my future husband. That following month, one of AJ 's best friends got married. AJ knew that I wanted to be married. We had been together as a couple for over five years. The first time I had seen my husband was in 2002; however, we officially met in in 2005. I remember him telling me the news of the new nuptials. Sitting on the couch, happy for the couple but tired of waiting on him to ask for my hand in marriage, I got up and proceeded to walk to our bedroom. He followed me in an attempt to comfort me in my sorrow of not being married. He said, " I know you want to be married…" but after those first seven words I zoned out. I did not want to hear any more excuses. I blankly nodded and said it was okay for him to leave me alone to go back doing whatever it was he was doing.

Days later I began reading my Bible more and more. Throughout the New Testament I constantly read how fornication was a sin. I had just made a commitment to God in serving Him spiritually for AJ to be made whole, so I felt convicted of living with this man, giving him my body without the commitment of marriage. Shortly after that I went to AJ and told him that if he did not want to get married that was fine; but we could no longer live together. I was going to move out of our home within two months.

The next morning, while he was at work, I woke up to a text message from him—asking for my hand in marriage. I was so elated. I was finally marrying the man of dreams.

On March 19, 2011 we got married in our living room before a group of only two people—the minister and his wife. Shortly after the ceremony, followed by the reception given to us by AJ's family, my mother decided she no longer wanted to be a mother. She had kicked out the remaining children living in her home, including my 11-year-old brother. Newly wed to my husband, we fought for custody of him because I had grown tired of my mother mistreating her children by neglecting them while living in her home. After filing court documents throughout the summer in hopes of receiving full custody of my sibling, the presiding judge instructed me to return my brother back to my mother's custody.

We were all devastated.

My mother stood in the court, lied to the judge (saying I had kidnapped her child) then sat outside the courtroom afterwards without saying a word to me. After the custody battle I began to focus more on my new life with my husband. We were only married for a little while before we fought for custody for my brother. I realized the heaviness that we would have to carry while raising a teenager at such a young age.

My mother later admitted that after the custody battle she realized being a mother was more important to her than she had thought. I guess there was something about being close to losing your children to caused the wake up call. She wanted to become a better mother so I initially backed off of from my family to allow room for my mother to grow as the primary caregiver.

My husband and I graduated from college in December 2012 and worked on a business adventure together. In January 2014, we were scheduled to move to Houston, Texas. Little did I know that would never come to pass.

During a beautiful, fall evening in October 2013, my husband was killed in a tragic car accident. I remember getting the phone call from the hospital asking me to come quickly and that my husband was in accident. I raced to the hospital and paced the floor, anxiously waiting to hear news from his surgery. The doctors told me when I arrived that he had broken bones and internal bleeding; therefore, they had to perform emergency surgery.

After signing all the appropriate documentation I waited to hear back. Time went on, I prayed. Time continued to go on, I continued to pray while staring at the clock. Friends and family began to arrive to keep me company as we waited to hear any news. Three hospital officials arrived asking for me. I stood up. The female physician informed me that my husband's surgery did not go well. They tried everything they could but they could not get him to come back. I stood there lifeless. Shocked. Completely blindsided. A trip that should have only lasted three hours ended with us being a lifetime apart. My husband was dead. He did not survive the car accident.

Even as I write this story, I'm still in shock.

I turned to God to help me face the reality of my situation and to help me overcome it. I gave myself two options that night. I could allow it to take me down, or I could overcome it so I could tell the world how God brought me through it. I had been through child neglect, putting myself through college, fighting racial discrimination on my job, a child custody battle with my mother, and now the death of my spouse.

I wasn't going to begin losing after overcoming so much.

So, I fought. I knew, due to the trauma, I could become addicted to any coping mechanism. My background in Health Education, studying drug education, taught me the various addictive mechanisms in which we as humans easily indulge. Since I was so broken, I did not want to fall prey to becoming dependent on something to help with the pain I was feeling within. So I fought without taking any prescription pills to cope with the sleepless nights or to ease the constant heartache I was feeling. I fought through my anguish, pain, loss, frustration and mental distress to the point of losing my mind, disappointment and trauma.

Through my journey of healing from the death of my husband, God revealed deep truths of the soul healing I needed from my previous life experiences. Some were from childhood, but many formed during adolescence; and in turn, shaped the personality I have today.

God showed me the person I truly am.

I now know how to analyze a situation and to pinpoint the root cause of a person's behavior. Losing my husband was the hardest thing I had ever gone through in life. It changed my life forever. My perception on life is different. Death can cause the lens of your soul to be gloomy and dark. Simple joys of life feel like a lifetime ago. A mask could not hide the truth. I found myself during my earthquake. Right after my husband's death, I searched for all kinds of research on Heaven, death, spiritual help, treatments, and anything to which I could relate. I found groups for widows with children, army widows, elderly widows, widows of middle age but none like me, a widow who was young without children. These groups offered group support but nothing on spiritual techniques to heal. I decided to form a ministry to help widows from all walks of life to heal properly from death and grief. In doing so, I have to share my story on the many experiences I had during my healing process. I learned

DREAMS . RESILIENCE . LOVE

that healing will only go as far as the person is willing to take it.

While healing, I discovered a lot of my perceptions had to do with the many situations I had formed in past times; thus, they had a lot to do with my reactions to the things that had transpired in current times. My mindset had to change in order to heal the many layers of hurt I had experienced. Therefore, the Foundation of Serenity Inc Ministry came to fruition via the Holy Spirit. It's a healing ministry that ushers deliverance from death and grief through transformation techniques.

I pray that my vulnerability in sharing such intimate moments of my life will shine light on the constant guiding hand of God in yours. God truly does love us. He really does heal the brokenness. You just have to be willing to allow God to shine light on the dark shadowy things in your life, use discipline, consistency and determination to achieve your healing. I'm not saying your healing journey will be easy. That would be a lie. What I am saying is if you hold onto God's unchanging hand, He will bring you through. He will give you strength when you are weak. When you feel like you cannot fight anymore, He will strategically place someone in your life to guide through that stage. Do not give up. Do not lose hope. For He truly knows how strong you are. He know your authentic you.

If God had told me, when I was child of all of things, what I would have experienced thus far, I would have told Him no thank you. I cannot do it. But I am still here. Standing strong. I made up my mind when I was twenty-five years old that I shall overcome this with blinded faith. I've gone through financial struggles, betrayals and breakage in relationships, slander and many more things. He has truly provided His power to me throughout all of my suffering. He is the author and finisher of all things.

No matter how bleak your path may seem, please, I beg you keep holding on and fighting for what is rightfully yours.

> "For I know the plans I have for you," declares the LORD, "plans to prosper you and not to harm you, plans to give you hope and a future."
> ~ Jeremiah 29:11

Chelsey Barton was born to Warren and Lillian Green and raised in Forrest City, Arkansas. She graduated from Forrest City High School in 2006 and later relocated to Little Rock Arkansas to earn her Bachelor of Science degree in Health Science with an emphasis on Health Education and Promotion and a Minor in Legal Studies. Chelsey married her husband of two and half years, Mr. Alvin (AJ) Barton, in March 2011. Their marriage was short lived, when at the tender age of 25, AJ died after a tragic car accident. Chelsey underwent a lot of social, economic and spiritual changes. Through the great loss of a spouse including dear relationships, financial stability, mental and spiritual peace, Chelsey found God in a great way.

My relationship with God changed my life for the greater. I did not realize how broken
I was until I was completely broken.
I lost my life but gained in greater ways.

FREEDOM

by Alexis Diane Finks

Sweat stung my eyes and my hands ached from picking cotton all day. My clothes were dirty and torn. I looked up to see the sunset. I put the rest of my cotton in my half-full basket and took a long, hard look at the fence that separated the outside world from us slaves. Suddenly, I heard the lashing of a whip and a loud cry. Master Edmonson was beating Auntie Jade. She cried for him to stop, but he just told her to shut up or he would kill her. Tears ran down her face as he pushed her to the ground.

"Work peasant." He spat.

I ran to Auntie Jade and tried to help her up, but she pushed me away.

"Child you'd better get back to work before he comes back and beats you too," she said, picking up her scattered cotton.

"I want to escape I want to be free!" I cried spreading my arms.

She shook her head. "We all want to be free child, but escaping is dangerous and I wouldn't want anything to happen to you."

"One day." I mumbled, walking back to my basket. "One day."

I picked up my basket and put it on the outside of the cottage. I walked in and the aroma of cooked potatoes and carrots filled the small cottage. Mamma was making her usual stew. I looked around for Poppa. He was usually late due to beatings or more work, but he never arrived after sunset.

"Momma, where is Poppa?"

She turned to me and frowned. She motioned for me to sit down as she sat in her rocking chair—my favorite chair. One of Master's daughters had snuck it into the cottage. She felt it wasn't right that we had to sleep and sit on the floor. That's just the way of life for us slaves, I had told her.

Momma sighed loudly, breaking my train of thought. "Olivia, you know that your Poppa loves us a lot."
I nodded. "Well he… he had to be sold. How could you let this happen?"

She gave me a look of despair and got up to continue cooking. I ran out the door, toward the fences. I looked at the woods and cried out loud. "I'm going to escape and no one is going to stop me!" I sighed and fell to the ground. Cotton brushed against my face. I closed my eyes and imagined the sound of freedom, the sight of freedom, the smell of freedom and the feel of freedom. It felt amazing.

I suddenly heard a whip in the air. The sound came closer and closer until it was directly behind me. I sat up and turned around to see Master with a leather whip in his hand and an angry look on his face.

"Why aren't you in your cottage peasant?" He growled.

FREEDOM

I tried to answer, but no words formed. He glared at me and started to raise his whip, then put it down immediately. "Get in that cottage `fore I whip you to death."

I nodded and ran to the cottage. I was confused as to why he didn't whip me, but I was grateful. Momma was pouring her stew into a broken bowl. She offered the bowl to me and I took it. I sat down and started drinking out of the bowl. It tasted brackish and bitter but it was just how I liked it. I finished my soup and changed for bed. We had no way to bathe, unless you count the nearby lake behind the fence. I changed into the same old, tattered nightgown that I'd had for as long as I could remember. I looked at my nightgown and frowned. I wish I had nice silk gowns like the Master's youngest daughter, Alexa. She was so beautiful with her nice ribbons tied in her hair and her skin shining like the sun.

I got under my quilt and looked at Momma. She snuggled underneath it with me. It was the only one Master Edmonson had given us. She sighed and kissed my cheek. Then, she blew out the oil lamp beside us. I couldn't sleep. All I could think about was when Master Edmonson didn't whip me. *Did he feel bad?* No he couldn't have. *White men… slave owners they… they didn't feel anything for slaves.* I looked over at Momma. She was fast asleep. Tired from work I guessed. I remembered before Master Edmonson came and I was looking at the fence—one step closer to freedom, one step closer to not ever having to work again. I wanted freedom. I sat up and started thinking.

"No one is awake… I would be able to escape," I thought out loud. But then there was Momma. I couldn't just leave her behind, but she wouldn't like the idea of us escaping in the middle of the night. I thought about it once more and decided I would escape that night.

I had no idea what I was getting myself into and I really didn't care. All I really cared about was freedom. I stood up, removing the quilt from my body and making sure I didn't wake Momma. I kneeled down and kissed her forehead.

"I will be back, Momma." I whispered.

I lit an oil lamp and walked out of the small cottage, taking in my surroundings. No one was out in the quiet night. It was pitch black with nothing but my oil lamp shining in the darkness—no crickets chirped, no rabbits thumped around. Everything and everyone was asleep, just as I should have been. But how could I sleep knowing my father could be dead? I walked up to the fence looking at the dark wood ahead of me. *I can do this.* I thought. *For Momma and Poppa.*

I threw my lantern over the tall fence. Its light still shined bright. I climbed over the fence and fell. I broke my arm, but otherwise I was okay. I picked up my lantern and kept on moving. My unstable shoes were not going to make the journey, so I just left them in a low bird's nest. I walked for what had seemed like hours when I heard a voice.

"Trying to escape, eh Slave?" The voice questioned as it got closer and closer. "Just give up now and you wont be killed."

I started running, weaving through the trees, trying to lose my hunter; but he always seemed to be right behind me. I found a pile of leaves and straw and quickly buried myself under them. I heard footsteps run past me and I was sure he was gone. I came up from all the leaves and continued walking. I walked near a stream and splashed my face with water. It was nearly sunrise when I saw a

FREEDOM

house with a quilt in front of a window. It seemed to be a safe place where I could rest until night came again. So, I knocked on the door and a caramel-skinned woman opened the door with a smile on her face.

"G... good morning," I shivered.

She frowned. "Oh child you must be freezing! Come in, come in."

She tended to my broken arm and let me rest until night. I thanked her for her help and I was on my way. I walked for hours and hours, until my body finally gave in and I passed out. I woke up in a nice bed with a woman looking at my arm. She was a white woman, but something told me she was not going to hurt me. I slowly sat up, trying not to move my arm. She looked at me and smiled.

"Good. You're awake. Some bounty hunters almost found you but luckily I came before they could reach you. Honey, you are a wanted slave. Is your owner rich?" She asked, looking at the window beside me.

"Yes… very wealthy." I answered my voice cracking.

She smiled. "Well, I'm Sara and I'm going to be helping you out. I've helped a lot of slaves escape; but you're my first child."

I nodded. I was in so much shock that she was white and helping me. *Was this a trick? How was I to know?*

She continued talking. She finally stood up and said something about making dinner. I nodded and followed her to the kitchen. I sat down and waited for her to serve me dinner. It was the best dinner I'd had in years. I was finishing up when I thought of Momma—all alone and worried that I was being beaten or worse. I stood up and started washing dishes. She smiled and took the sponge out of my hands gently.

"I'll wash the dishes. You rest." She said as she started washing.

I went into the room and went back to my bed and thought about the few people who cared about me. I thought about Auntie Jade and how she must be worried sick. I thought about Poppa who was probably being worked harder than ever. I wanted to go back and get all my family and bring them to this nice, kind woman; but I knew she would not like me going back out into the woods.

I stayed in Sara's home for weeks, almost months, and I never worked. It was just like I imagined freedom, only I was with someone I barely knew and not with my family. But Sara cared about me as if I were her daughter. She never got angry with me, and she always comforted me when I missed my family. I woke up one day to Sara panicking and pacing around the room.

"Sara, what's the matter?" I asked.

She looked at me as if she were going to cry. "Oh Olivia! Its horrible!"

I stood up and tried to calm her down.
"Slow down Sarah. What's going on?"

She took a deep breath and sat down on a blue chair in the corner of the small room.

FREEDOM

"My husband is coming today." She said with a look of sadness on her face.

I looked over at her confused. "But isn't that a good thing?" She shook her head. "No, no, no. I was planning to keep you until… well I don't know but he's a slave hunter and he will definitely find you."

I knew it! I knew it was way too good to be true! A white… help me? Yeah, sure. I narrowed my eyes as I tried to think of a plan, but nothing came to me. Then I heard the creak of a door and a deep hearty voice.

"Sara, honey. I'm home!" He called.

She panicked and ran into the kitchen. "Find any of those filthy slaves?" I heard her say. I wasn't offended. I had heard that a lot.

"No, sadly all the filthy little rats are all behaving."

"Well I must be getting dinner started." She said nervously.

I peeked around the door and saw a big man blocking my view of almost all the kitchen. The man slowly turned around and spotted me. I quickly closed the door. I saw a glimpse of his fat face, his mouth curled up into a wicked smile. He opened the door with the same wicked smile upon his face.

"Well, it looks like we got the first slave of the day."

Alexis Diane Finks lives in Duluth, Georgia, where she attends Berkeley Lake Elementary. Her fifth grade teacher is Miss Blackburn. Alexis first developed an interest in writing in the third grade. She is an avid reader and honors student. She participates in the Berkeley Lake Chorus and is one of only four students who were selected to sing in the Honors Chorus. Alexis attends Eagles Nest Church in Roswell, Georgia. She is three-year member of the Eagles Nest Dance Ministry. She also participates in Teen Ministry Productions and Praise and Worship. Her parents are Adrian and Shana Finks. She has two older sisters, Ariel and Sydney Finks. Alexis aspires to pursue a career in writing.

SCHOOL DAYS

by Phyllis Hodges

My childhood was the best. I felt fortunate to have three brothers and a sister. We were all so close, about a year apart in age. Our mother didn't work outside the home until we all were in school. We were products of the Little Rock Public School District. These were neighbor schools, all in walking distance from our home on Chester Street. Schools were segregated during those times; our elementary school went from K- 6th Grade. During our daily walk to school, we would always see our friends along the route. Rightsell Elementary School was less than a block from our Junior High School. School was fun, most of the time, because I had a lot of friends and I found myself being the ringleader of most of our activities.

I think back and laugh. I was a leader with quality leadership skills even then. I had several teachers I admired; and most of them lived in the neighborhood as well. Mrs. Sue Cowan Williams, one of my English teachers, was a remarkable history maker. Mrs. Williams didn't only make a difference in my life, but she was instrumental in changing the lives of most African Americans teachers.

During those days the Parent Teacher Association (PTA) was very important to most families. My mom was very active in our early years in our schools. She would volunteer in our classrooms, go on field trips, and serve through many positions on the PTA Board.

My Junior High School, which was segregated, spanned 7th-9th Grade. Dunbar Junior High School was the school most African Americans in Little Rock remember attending. There were not many schools for African Americans during those times. This phase of my life as a Junior High student was a bit nerve racking because as a 7th grader coming to a school where the majority of students were older and bigger; and that was a bit frightening.

Sixth grade was the highest level in my elementary school; so I thought I was really in charge. But since 7th grade was the lowest grade at the big junior high school, I was very intimidated. I had to learn how to change classes, and how to use lockers. Everything was so new to me.

During junior high I was enrolled in a typing class, something that I hated. It was because of this vain spirt my mother said I had. I had long beautiful nails that I was required to cut. Of course, I didn't want to do that; so I didn't apply myself. I was introduced to calculators, cash registers, typewriters and other clerical items in the class. That was way before computers and modern technology.

But what made me smile was knowing I was at a school with everyone from the neighborhood. We were like a big happy family. My two older siblings, Pam and James, were there with me. My two younger siblings, Tony and Terry, were in the age bracket where the school district started to integrate the schools. That meant we had to bus our neighborhood families across town. I didn't understand it. Most families where uncomfortable with it, but we had to adjust.

The new schools—Brady Elementary, Mitchell Elementary, Pulaski Heights Middle and other schools—popped up all over town.

SCHOOL DAYS

Integration had started and we began attending schools with white children. My two younger brothers and many of our friends where caught in this change. They had to get up early, and stand on the corner to ride the school buses. This was a new experience for many accustomed to walking to neighborhood schools. Unfortunately, we were a bit confused because these big school buses passed right by the neighborhood schools where some of the neighborhood kids still attended. Plus a lot of families, like ours, were affected because of the split with some older siblings attending the neighborhood schools and the younger siblings being bused out of the neighborhoods. This process was disturbing because families and friends where now being divided by street addresses which determined the schools that students attended.

Now about Dunbar: my Dad got involved during my junior high years. As always, I was very active in clubs, sporting events, dance teams and beauty contests. As a matter of fact, there was one beauty pageant, *Miss Spirit of Cotton*, in which the criteria to win was based on who raised the most money. My Dad, James Marshall Sr., was an old- school entrepreneur. All he knew was working for himself, making money and providing for his family.

We discussed the contest and he assured me that he would help me win. I knew then that I would be *Miss Spirit of Cotton of Dunbar Junior High*. Dad went the extra mile to help me sell ads. He went to every business person in town, African American and Caucasian. He went to family members and strangers, it didn't matter if he knew them or not, he was going to help me win the pageant. By the end of the pageant, dad didn't know if he had assisted in helping me raise enough ad money or not; so he decided to add his own hard earned money. Now I can say my first title was *Miss Spirit of Cotton of Dunbar Junior High*.

I was very outspoken during my school years. Sometimes my mouth would get me in trouble. The roles of my parents would switch. I remember how active my mom was in school during my elementary years, but dad became more active in my junior high years. Mom, was a no nonsense woman and had very little tolerance for the dumb stuff. So when I would get in trouble and a teacher conference would be called, Dad would have to be the one to attend. My choices and my poor behavior lead to difficult consequences.

Dunbar is where I bonded with my closest friend, Gwen, from the neighborhood. Forty years later, she is still one of my best friends. I had lots of friends, girls and boys. We all lived in the same neighborhood and were like family. Our neighborhoods were so nice, quiet and safe. We played outside until it was dark. We went from house to house and we would walk the whole entire block without feeling afraid of anybody. Mom would even walk to the stores with us. She would play outside games with us.

Life growing up was so much fun. Mom even allowed us to have sleepovers known as "bunkin parties" and she would even agree to let us attend a few of our friends' sleepovers, as long as she knew their parents. Families weren't so afraid of cruel things happening in the private homes as we witness today.

As a matter of fact, I remember when Mom agreed to allow my sister Pam to attend a weekend, overnight event sponsored by the Y-teens. Once a year the fair would come to town and Mom and one of her lady friends would get all their children and we would get together—walking from Chester Street all the way down to Roosevelt Road to the Arkansas State Fair. Again, we wouldn't be

SCHOOL DAYS

afraid of any kind of bad things happening. It was just unheard of. When you think about drive by shootings, kidnapping or murders, it was so different back then. As they say, "the good ole days."

My senior high days were in the seventies at Hall High School—an experience of a lifetime. I took the bus to school since all school districts had become integrated. My friends and I took several classes together, we all made decent grades. I served as a statistician for the basketball team—a very unique position. Most of the girls wanted to be a cheerleader or a dancer on the school's dance team. I desired much more and wanted to be a leader in organizations. In this case, our basketball team was receiving national notoriety because Sidney Moncrief was one of our lead players. I definitely wanted to be apart of a history making moment, and basketball challenged so many youth to strive high.

We all became mentors and role models. I was also a member of the FBLA (Future Business Leaders of America) and FHA (Future Homemakers of American); plus I volunteered to assist elementary school students. One of the highlights was when the Arkansas Democrat-Gazette (formally known as the Arkansas Gazette) came out to highlight the story of a high school student mentoring other children. A few days later, a picture of the children and me appeared in the paper. I was fortunate enough to be able to attend school half of the day, because I had enough credits to graduate. So I got my first part time job at the age of sixteen at KFC (Kentucky Fried Chicken), where I met a faithful customer who became my soul mate. Byron Hodges was a junior at UALR, and the rest of my school days are history.

Phyllis Hodges wears many hats and expresses many gifts and talents, so she goes by many names—Mrs. Hodges, Mom, Dearest, Minister Phyl, Dr. Phyl, Master Fitness Trainer Phyl and the list goes on. Phyllis is a native of Little Rock, Arkansas and a product of public schools: Rightsell Elementary, Dunbar Junior High and Hall High School. Other schools and universities include Missionary Baptist Seminary, Agapa College (formally ASWE Laymen School) and Full Counsel School Of World Evangelism. She worked as a television personality and producer/creator of her own talk show, 30-Plus at BET 14, KASN 38 and KATV 7. Later she worked as a fitness personality for KARK 4 and FOX 16. Phyllis served six years working for the city of Little Rock as the Assistant Director and then for War Memorial Fitness Center (now known as Jim Dailey Fitness and Aquatics Center). Following that she was hired as the city's Fitness Specialist. Following her extensive career, in 2000 she opened her own business: Carousel Fit 4 Life Wellness Center, the first and only faith-based health and wellness Center. Phyllis started her writing career in 2001 to expand the vision of her business and to help shape up the world spiritually, mentally, physically and financially. She self-published her first book: "A Divine Connection." Her next two books were love stories titled, "I Founded a Man" and a history book titled "8 Years of Unforgettable History," which will be published by Butterfly Typeface Publishing House.

Phyllis and her husband Byron have two adult children and three grandchildren. Phyllis's hero is her mom, Mama Rose. Phyllis can be reached via social media under Phyllis Hodges or Carousel Fit 4 Life Wellness Center.

VISITING MOTHER

by Jonelle Grace Lipscomb

The elevator door shut heavily, closing us inside the stale-smelling box that would take us to the third floor of the St. Louis State Mental Hospital. As I stood back and watched the floors pass by the small window above my head, I was careful not to touch anything. I wasn't sure why Mother was in the hospital. Grandmom said she got sleeping sickness when she was little, and it made her nervous, and sometimes she'd lose her temper. I thought maybe it had something to do with my father leaving.

Once during recess at school, a girl I didn't like much said, "My mother told me your mother's crazy."

That night, I asked Grandmom if Mother was crazy, and she said, "I don't want to ever hear you use that word again. Do you understand?"

Mother was in a closed ward because she had hit another patient, so we rang the bell and waited to be let in. A nurse's face pressed up against the bar-covered square of glass, and the thick door swung open.

"I bet you're here to see Maxey Lee. She's been talking about you all week." She bent over and put her big arms on her knees. "You must be her little girl. Your mother has an awfully pretty picture of you in her room." She smiled really big, so I smiled too, and she let us in.

As we walked down the hall, our steps echoed like gunshots on the hard linoleum floor, and some of the patients came out and stood in the doorways to watch us pass. One of them donned a Santa hat, and another wore a headband with reindeer antlers on top. We were almost to the end of the hall when I saw Mother coming. With her hands on her hips and her elbows jutting out, she looked like a fat mother duck waddling along. I stiffened as she threw her arms around me, but hugged her back, smelling the odor from under her arms. Finally, she let go and hugged Grandmom. "Come on, I want you to meet my friend Mable."

"Snooky, we don't have a lot of time today," Grandmom said, but Mother wasn't listening. She took my hand and led me into Mable's room. Mable was sitting by the window, but stood up when we walked in. "This is my Jonelle. Isn't she beautiful? She's eight years old."

Mable smiled and started to cry. She was so thin you could see her bones under her skin, and the tears ran down her face, making little pools in the hollows of her cheeks. Then, right in the middle of crying, she began to laugh, a thin, high little laugh, and held me close to her. Mother laughed and held me, too. Mother's arms were big and heavy, but I could hardly feel Mable's arms at all. The big nurse was standing in the doorway smiling; and when Mable and Mother quit laughing, she stepped into the room.

"Maxey Lee's told all her friends that you play the piano. Won't you play a few songs for them before you go?"

Grandmom looked down. "Jonelle, what do you tell her?"

"Yes, Ma'am," I said as Mother took my hand.

VISITING MOTHER

We went to the group room, where the patients were all gathered. I played my Bach sonata and Chopin nocturne on the piano. The patients smiled and clapped after each, and closed around me in a tight circle when I finished playing.

Grandmom signed us out to go shopping. I didn't like going out because Mother looked funny. Her loose jersey dress hung formless on her stocky body; and her shapeless, permed hair was pushed straight back from her face with a plastic headband. Grandmom made her put in her false teeth, but Mother kept complaining, pushing them around with her tongue and making little sucking sounds.

Usually, when we went downtown, we rode the bus; but today we drove. We were going to Styx Baer & Fuller, and it was easier to get there by car. Mother knew exactly which streets to take and their names from when she wasn't in the hospital. Grandmom knew which way to go, but she pretended that she didn't so Mother could tell her.

"Your mother was such a smart little girl," Grandmom said. "She can remember anything."

I was busy looking up at the sky. "I hope it snows."

"Be careful what you wish for," Grandmom said.

When we got to Styx Baer & Fuller there were so many cars we had to park on the far edge of the lot. As we walked down the row of cars, Mother kept trying to hold my hand, but I pulled away and ran all the way to the door. When they caught up with me, I was out of breath from running and stomping my feet on the concrete walk to keep warm. Mother's face was red as a beet. "You shouldn't run through parking lots," she yelled. "Don't you know you could get hit by a car?" A few tiny flakes of snow fell lightly on my face.

"It's too cold to walk," I said and pushed through the big revolving door.

Mother was hungry, so we went to the snack bar first. It was crowded when we got there, and we had to wait fifteen minutes for a booth. I ordered a hamburger with extra pickles, and Grandmom always asked for pecan pie and coffee. Mother ordered a big lunch of fried chicken, mashed potatoes and a lot of other things. As soon as the waitress left, Mother started rubbing her hands together, slipping her fingers in and out like when you play "Here's a church and here's a steeple." The first thing she always did when she got nervous was rub her hands. Grandmom looked at Mother.

"Snooky, why don't you take Jonelle to the lady's room to wash up for lunch?"

Mother didn't answer. Her glasses had slipped down her nose. She pushed them up with her finger and turned to the waitress, who was clearing the dishes from the booth next to us. "Is our food ready yet?"

The waitress smiled and said, "We're awfully busy, but it shouldn't take much longer."

Grandmom took a book from her purse. "I was going to give this to you when we got back, but you can read it now if you like."

Mother opened the book. I knew what Grandmom would say next,

VISITING MOTHER

and she did. "Your mother was always the best reader in her class. That's where you get it from."

Mother started reading, but every time the waitress came by our booth, she asked about our food. Mother must have asked at least four times, and after a while, the waitress quit smiling. Suddenly, Mother slammed the book down on the tabletop and stood up.

Grandmom looked at her and said in a voice as even as if she had beaten it out on a drum. "Maxey Lee, sit down."

Mother didn't say anything. She just stood with her hands on the back of her hips. I stared at the big damp circles under her arms. Then, she looked straight at Grandmom. "I'm going to the kitchen and get our food." She started to walk away, but Grandmom stood up and grabbed her arm. "Let me go," Mother yelled and jerked away. They both stood there frozen. The whole snack bar was quiet. Even the waitress who had been making a bunch of noise cleaning the tables stopped. I was afraid Mother might do something like the time she came to visit us in Arkansas.

We were all in the kitchen helping with supper. It was so hot my t-shirt was stuck to my back, and I was holding it out over the fan to get cool. Mother made the salad. I guess she was hot, too, because she wiped her face with her arm, walked over to the icebox and took out the milk. Then, she pushed the door closed with her foot. She didn't get a glass or anything; she just lifted the lid off the bottle and took three big swallows. Grandmom looked up and then turned back to the stove.

"Maxey Lee, please pour your milk into a glass."

Mother looked at Grandmom and took two more swallows. There wasn't a sound in the kitchen except for the fan. Grandmom walked to the icebox and stopped. "Maxey Lee, give me the milk."

Mother lowered the bottle. "No."

Grandmom froze like a statue. Mother froze too, and so did I. We all three just stood there like we had been playing slinging statues and had to freeze where we stopped. Then, everything came unfrozen at once. Grandmom jerked the bottle away from Mother; and when she did, milk spilt all over them both. I started laughing at them standing there covered with milk until Mother grabbed Grandmom's shoulders and started shaking her. Grandmom had long grey hair that she wore in a bun; but Mother pulled it down, and it was flying all around. The bottle shattered on the floor. Mother kept screaming, "I hate you," and Grandmom was crying. I started crying, too, and then Granddad came in and pulled them apart.

"Sorry to keep you waiting," the waitress said, and stood there with our food until Mother and Grandmom sat down.

After we finished eating, we went shopping. It was a huge toy department. Where I lived in Arkansas, all we had was a five and dime. But, Eureka Springs was a lot smaller than St. Louis. In fact, it was the smallest town I knew of in Arkansas, except maybe for those little towns with only a grocery store that you passed between real towns. We couldn't stay long, though, because Mother was only signed out until six.

It was dark when we stepped out of the store, and all the lights on the poles were on. Grandmom couldn't remember on which row we

VISITING MOTHER

had parked, and I hadn't noticed either because I'd been running. Mother knew, though. She said, "It's on Row C at the end." Mother was good at remembering things like that.

It was colder when we got out of the car, and the flakes of snow were falling faster. They were the big, flat kind. I kept my head tilted back all the way to the hospital door and watched the flakes get bigger right before they touched my face and turned into drops of water. I even caught two flakes on my tongue. Mother was quiet all the way up the elevator. But, when Grandmom rang the bell for the nurse, she said, "I don't want to go back yet. I'll be good. I promise I'll be good."

Grandmom stared straight ahead at the little window in the door. "We have to go to a dinner tonight, Snooky. We'll be back tomorrow."

Mother began to cry; and when the nurse opened the door, she pushed past her. When we went into her room, she was sitting on the bed. I couldn't see her face because she was looking out the window, but I could tell she was still crying because her shoulders shook every now and then. Her teeth were lying on the floor next to the bed. Grandmom picked them up and put them on the dresser and sat down on the bed next to Mother.

"Snooky, you don't want Jonelle to see you cry."

Mother's shoulders trembled, and then they were still. Mother turned and threw her big arms tight around Grandmom's neck and held her. Her shoulders shook again as she cried. "I'm sorry, Mother. I love you, and I want to be good; but I hate it here. I want to go home."

WRITING OUR LIVES

"I know, Snooky, I know," Grandmom said softly and smoothed Mother's hair with her hand. The plastic headband fell out and made a clattering sound as it hit the linoleum floor. Grandmom put her arms around Mother's back and rocked slowly back and forth until Mother's shoulders quit trembling and everything was still in the room.

"Snooky," Grandmom said, "tell Jonelle goodbye now because we have to go."

Mother turned and held out her arms. I sat down on the bed, and she pulled me close, pressing her face against mine. Her skin was soft and wet from the tears. "Promise me you'll write me more," she said.

"I promise."

"I love you. You're the best little girl anyone could ever have."

"I love you too," I lied.

Her heavy arms smothered me into her chest, and I could feel her breasts heaving softly under the loose jersey dress. I pulled out of her arms and kissed her cheek. "Goodbye, Mommy." I turned and walked out of the room without looking back. When I came out the door, I must have surprised the nurse because she jumped. "Would you let me out, please?" I asked.

As I followed her down the hall, I watched my feet click across the floor and tried not to touch the lines between the squares. I didn't want to look at the patients standing in the doorways. Some of them didn't blink. They just stared like pictures. When we reached

VISITING MOTHER

the end of the hall, the big nurse opened the heavy door.

"Would you please tell my grandmother that I've gone to the car?"

She smiled. "Sure, honey. Come visit your mother again real soon. She misses you very much."

"Yes Ma'am," I said and went out the door.
It was cold when I got outside and snowing hard. The flakes came so fast it was like flying through them; and when I looked up, I felt dizzy. I squatted close to the sidewalk and watched the snow pile up on my shoes. As the flakes landed, I could see the pattern of each one on the shiny black patent leather for just a moment, before it melted and trickled down the sides of my shoes onto the white covered ground. When I stood, and turned around, I could hardly see the hospital through the snow. On the third floor, a light went out. It was the only room that was dark, like a big neon sign with one bulb broken.

I turned away. The rows of cars were asleep under thick white quilts, and the only sound was the padded whisper of snow. I ran to our car, opened the door, and slipped inside. It was like crawling into a snow cave; but when I closed the door, a piece of white fell away leaving a hole. I watched the opening grow smaller until only a tiny circle remained. I pressed my face against the glass, took a deep breath, and let it out slowly. When my breath cleared, there was only snow.

Jonelle Grace Lipscomb is a writer, filmmaker, director, actress and educator. She holds a B.S.E. in Speech and Drama and a M.A. in Theatre and Communication from the University of Arkansas and a M.F.A. in Playwriting from the University of Georgia. After returning to Arkansas in 1991, Jonelle spent ten years as a Teaching Artist with the Arkansas Arts Council, Arts Live Theatre, and Walton Arts Center. During this time, she created a dozen original plays, six of which toured statewide. In 2000, excerpts from two plays were included in Scenes and Monologues for Young Actors, published by Dramatic Publishing. Jonelle was awarded an Individual Artist Fellowship in playwriting from the Arkansas Arts Council in the fall of 2001. She taught drama and filmmaking at Fayetteville High School from 1999 to 2014, during which time she began an award-winning film program. Now retired, Jonelle remains involved in writing, directing, and performing.

THE HOUSE AT THE END OF THE WORLD

by Jean Hicks McIntosh

My first memories are of dirt, dust and trees—dirt under the front porch, dirt in the front yard, even the road is all dirt and dust that floats across the front yard and into the house. I am riding my tricycle around and around on the front porch. My grandfather watches over me, making sure I do not roll off the three-foot high plank porch. My grandmother, mother and aunt are in the living room listening to "Helen Trent," a five minute soap opera that airs Monday through Fridays at 11:55am, on the radio.

The house sat at the end of the world. At least that it is how I perceived it at the age of four. One would have to travel to the small town of Strong, Arkansas in South Arkansas, eighteen miles south of El Dorado, Arkansas on Highway 82, turn right at the four way stop sign, right on Aurelle Road through the smaller community of Pine Grove to the first left, Monument Road and onto a dirt road into the smaller settlement of Free Hope, headed toward the state line. About two miles down a dirt road sat a house on a foundation of concrete blocks. The house was the last vestige of human population in the state of Arkansas, several miles into the state Louisiana.

I slow my tricycle and lean down to watch a mother hen and her six biddies resting in the dirt under the porch. I make plans to chase them as soon as my brother Jimmy and cousin Johnny wake from their naps. In the back of my four-year-old mind I am also thinking of the switching I will get from my grandmother for chasing the mother hen and her babies, if I am discovered. I usually plan my chasing when she is visiting or at a church meeting. She had made it clear that under no circumstance her setting hens, mother hens or their biddies are to be chased, period.

Across the dirt road, pine trees stand tall reaching for the clear blue sky. The Persimmon trees sway in the slow breeze, loaded down with orange fruit. Oak trees, their branches moving graceful in the breeze, march on each side of the dirt road to the Louisiana state line and beyond. Crepe Myrtles stand guard on both sides of the gate opening into the front yard covered in brown dirt sweep clean—not a blade of grass or weed is visible.

The house is small but well built. A large living room faces the front porch. Two bedrooms adjoin the living room, both on the right. Each bedroom is furnished with two beds and a dresser. The living room has a large bed covered in a colorful home-stitched quilt and white pillows. A dresser sits on the far wall, a wooden bench with another quilt draped across it, wooden straight back chairs are scattered around the room. A wood-burning heater resting on a sheet of tin metal sits on the wall shared with the front porch to the left of the front door. A large window opens onto the front porch with a Singer sewing machine resting under it. Screens on doors and windows keep bugs and flying insects at bay, but not the dust. The dining room and kitchen run across the back of the house. The dining room holds a long table with benches on each side and a white icebox. Ice is delivered twice a week. Natural light filters into the kitchen through a long rectangle window. Under the window sits a rough wooden table with a white tin dishpan and an another for rinsing. Two shelves under the table hold the pots and pans. Three steps across the room a wooden table covered in an oil tablecloth and three chairs provide the only seating in the room.

THE HOUSE AT THE END OF THE WORLD

A white cabinet sits in a corner. Dishes, cups, saucers and drinking glasses sit on the shelves. Knives, forks and spoons are stored in mason jars on the shelves with the dishes. Lower drawers hold dishcloths. Large stirring spoons, ladles and a piercing forks hang on the wall near a four- burner wood-burning stove with a stove pipe venting through the outside wall.

I still remember the homemade biscuits that came out of that stove each morning.

My grandmother steps out on the front porch and looks directly at my grandfather, "Hal be coming by in a few minutes. Will you get the mail? I need to get dinner on the table. The boys be here soon, and they'll be hungry."

"Be glad to," my grandfather replies as my grandmother turns to leave the porch. "Rains a coming," he says, headed down the stairs to wait for old Hal at the mailbox. I take a deep breath and smell the sweet approach of dampness in the air as grit enters my mouth and settles down my throat. The wind is no longer a gentle breeze. No chasing biddies, I think, but there is always tomorrow or the next day.

The road and front yard turn into a brown muddy mess if it rains for any length of time. Hal better hurry up and deliver that mail or he won't get here today and maybe not even tomorrow. The wind blows harder now. First it's just a breeze but five minutes later, just as Hal pulls off from the mailbox and my grandfather is back on the porch, the first drop of rain falls on the porch and the wind temporary loses its mind. The back door slams shut. My father and cousin are in from the field. Lunch is on the table, and I am hungry.

When my mother places a drumstick on my plate I wonder which of the chickens have been sacrificed today. Did it bother me? Not one bit. We had to eat and, I knew where all the food came from. The cabbage and potatoes came from my grandmother's garden out the back door and a short walk up a small incline. The blackberries for the cobbler came from a patch at the edge of the woodlands that occupied the land straight out the back door, through the grassy backyard and down a well-worn path on the other side of the pond. Four pecan trees provided shade in the large, grassy back yard.

The hog pen sat across the dirt road, in front of the house. At least two were killed each fall at hog killing time. Bacon, sausage, ham, pork chops, roast, fat back, chitterlings, fat for cooking, pork skins for snacking, and even soap came from the animals. Pig feet and pig ears were pickled. The cow pen also sat across the road near the hog pen. From the cows came milk and butter. If the cows were ever slaughtered, I have no memory of such happening.

Canning was done all summer and into the fall, as vegetables were harvested from the garden. Every inch of space under the beds held a canned item. Salt, sugar, flour purchased in fifty pound colorful cloth bags, corn meal, baking powder and soda were purchased at the Bennett Grocery Store on the Aurelle Road. Molasses and sugar cane syrup for biscuits and pancakes came from Uncle Genie's farm, a short walk through the woods. Fish appeared on the table once a week in the spring and summer and early fall. Ducks, squirrels and venison added variety in late fall and winter.
The rain continued for the rest of the day and long into the night. Sure enough there was a muddy mess the next two days. I knew I would get a switching for playing in the mud. I could just hear my mother's shrill voice as she viewed the mud in my hair. She hated washing my hair. All the women in my father and mothers family

THE HOUSE AT THE END OF THE WORLD

had long, straight or curly hair. Mine was neither. It was long, thick and nappy. The care of my hair took time; and time was something my mother did not want to devote to my hair. I am not talking about an hour or two. Three hours to wash, comb out the kinks and couch plaits in a four-year-old's hair was a bit much when the endless dusting, makings, daily weeding of the gardening, laundry and ironing had to be done by hand. This was the late forties. My hair took up almost a half of her day on a Saturday.

I now understand why it was an ordeal when I got dirt, mud or grit in my hair.

The next day I made up my mind. Switching or no switching, I was playing in the dirt. Jimmy and Johnny had no problem joining me. I was more careful than both of them. I stuck to mud cakes and left splashing, wading and mud fights to them. The end was a good scolding and a trip to the well with a bucket of water, cup-by-cup, poured over my already plaited hair. My mother was happy, and so was I, as I did not enjoy the care that my hair required.

Two days later I decided it was time to chase biddies. My grandmother did believe that a good switch could get a child's attention. She had told me many times if she ever caught me chasing her biddies or bothering her setting hens I would get a good switching. Two days after the rain, while Jimmy and Johnny were down for a nap and my grandfather was in the fields with my father and cousin, I decided it was time to chase biddies. As soon as the music announcing Helen Trent could be heard on the radio, I was on my way under the house. I did not have to crawl under the house. I just walked under, spotted the biddies and hen, and provoked them to run. I knew I could not get too close. I had to make sure there was always sufficient room between the mother hen and me. If not, I would lose some of my hair and suffer scratches in my head and on my face. This was not the first time I had played this game.

I chased them to the well, in and out of the chicken house, back to the house and back to the well. All this time they were squawking bloody murder. I was chasing them to the chicken house when my grandmother appeared with a long switch in her hand. She whipped that switch across my legs; and I felt hot, searing pain. The look on her face was not kind. She whipped that switch again, and I screamed bloody murder. She did not miss a beat. She whipped it again and my legs felt the hot, searing pain again. Two more and she was finished; and then she spoke. "What have I told you 'bout chasing my biddies and hens? Stop that crying. You knew exactly what was going to happen to you, but you did it anyway. Now shut your mouth and get in the house so I can wash those legs and put some salves on them. Next time you chase my biddies it will be eight whips." My grandmother never delivered punishment unless she had stated the punishment for disobedience.

I want to report that I have not one scar on my legs from the switching nor did I ever chase my grandmother's biddies and hens again.

I will never forget the house at the end of the world. The next summer, my parents moved us to the Gardner Community where my siblings and me would attend school from the first through the twelve grades. I visited the house at the end of the world most weekends and each summer until about the sixth grade. There were many adventures. Visiting the cow pasture near the hog pen to see a new born calf, seeing my mother's excitement as she learned to drive a log truck, waking up on an early fall morning and sneaking out of the house to go hunting with my cousin—only to discover

THE HOUSE AT THE END OF THE WORLD

the moonshine steel where the men of the small community were gathered around a barn fire drinking and laughing just having a good time—getting lost in the woods with my cousin, seeing cotton for the first time and lasting all of ten minutes in my only attempt to pick cotton. Trees surrounded The House at the End of the World. There were no huge farms with cotton, beans or wheat. The communities in that area were all dedicated to serving the pulp wood industry. There were a few small truck farms, but wood was king.

The House at the End of the World has long disappeared into history and memory. Its location can only be found by the long crepe myrtle bush that still stands guard where the gate used to be. I recently visited the area with two of my siblings and a cousin. We found the site the house formally occupied, and my sister Linda commented on the stillness and the sense of peace that still exist at the site.

As I grow older I see the house clearly in my memories, sometimes I think I still smell the biscuits and see my grandmother sitting at her churn, churning away to make butter. I see the special quilt my grandmother gave me to take to the garden so I could rest if I got tired while helping her pull weeds or pick vegetables from her garden. I can see my grandfather's smile and hear his laughter when I first discovered the true taste of black coffee.

Many lessons were learned in The House at the End of the World. Much laughter entered the house, and sometimes I would feel the house hugging me with all the love that poured from its walls.

Jean Hicks was born in Strong, Arkansas, and graduated from A.M. & N. College with a B.A. and a Master of Social Work from the University of Arkansas. During an illustrious thirty-three-year career in state government, she developed the first Foster Parent Recruitment Campaign in Jefferson County, which was later developed into a statewide campaign for recruiting Foster Parents. She also developed a volunteer training program for welfare mothers and one of the first family daycare organizations in Pulaski County. The Sisters of Color Book Club recognized Jean's short story, *The Gift*, and her second short story, *Rissa's Heart*, received encouraging reviews. Jean recently completed her first novel, *Free Hope*, and is doing research for another novel, *Children of the Most High God*.

Jean is the mother of a daughter, Shania, a son, Brandon and the grandmother of six.

WASHTUBS AND EMPTY LOTS

by David Nickell

Her small house sat on an equally small lot on the southeast side of the small town of Allen, Oklahoma. It was anything but fancy; however it boasted some of the most beautiful flowers, shrubs and other foliage in town. During the spring and summer months, you barely noticed the weathered siding, leaning fences and dilapidated porch. Within walking distance of my house, as a teenager I often visited Clara Gardner's humble home. I was her gardener. She was my friend.

As a young man finishing my last two years of high school, I was shy and didn't make friends easily; therefore, I had only a few close friends. Our family was new to the community and most of my classmates had gone to school together since kindergarten. They were never unkind, but I never felt the close connection to any of them that they seemed to share with one another.

For that reason, church became an important part of my life. My siblings, cousins and I made up the "youth group." Although our church was small, there was always something going on, and everyone was usually included—even the senior citizens.

One such "senior saint" was Clara Gardner. In her late seventies, with a shaky voice and stooped frame, she was your typical church lady. She attended regularly, baked cakes for potlucks and often stood up in church to "testify," and you just knew she probably prayed regularly for everybody in the church. I had somehow managed to inherit my father's deep respect for older folks and loved being around them, listening to their stories and eating their food.

Sis Gardner, as we church members called her, appreciated my attention. At some point, she needed a young man to help her with her yard, so she hired me for two dollars an hour. The pay wasn't much, but what I received from her on those spring and summer afternoons far surpassed the satisfaction of a little pocket change. She taught me things that I didn't even begin to understand until many years later. I learned about hospitality, pride in the little things God sends our way, and how poverty doesn't have to create barriers or chasms. I also learned that friendships often arise from just being a good listener.

On those sunny spring and summer afternoons, Sis Gardner would meet me at the door with a soft, quivery voice. "Hello, David." She crinkled her grey eyes into a smile, and I would lean over for a soft hug. Then she was all business.

She took immense pride in her yard, and she was picky. We would do a walk-through and she would establish what were weeds and what were flowers and would expect me to remember for future workdays. After we made the rounds, she left me to my work. I would watch her putter around the small yard for a few minutes before retreating into the tiny house, and then I proceeded to the east side of the house where the aging push mower sat waiting for me. She insisted that I always use her mower. Every season she had it serviced; and because there was no covered building in which to store it, a #2 washtub became its shelter. I mowed a lot of yards, but this was a first. I was always amazed that the old mower never failed to start. This odd choice of shelter was a strong example to me of

WASHTUBS AND EMPTY LOTS

the value in taking care of the things you are given, even if it isn't much.

I would lift the washtub off the mower, give it a crank and soon the small yard would begin to take shape. I carefully mowed around and under snowball shrubs, azaleas and rhododendrons. After mowing, I would go outside of the fence and weed around all the irises, lilies and other vibrant flowers that grew along the west side of the property near the road. It was important to me that she was pleased with my work because I knew how much the yard meant to her. She had very little in the way of possessions, but her pride in what she did have was evident. Once again, my father's convictions about the value of the elderly influenced my actions.

Meanwhile, in the tiny kitchen, Sis Gardner would shuffle about in a flowered house dress preparing small dishes of food for us to share after I finished the mowing and weeding: black-eyed peas, okra, stewed tomatoes and fried potatoes. There was never an abundance of anything but always plenty for the two of us.

Sometimes I would finish my chores before she had it prepared, and after making sure the mower was secured in its place in the side yard with the washtub on top, I would enter the back door and sit at the old-fashioned Formica table, sip cold water and watch her in her element.

Those times sitting with her at the kitchen table or in the small living room were moments that I cherish even today. She would ask me about school or what the youth group at church was planning. She inquired about my family and sometimes talked about her beloved Elmer, who had died many years before, and her alcoholic son who lived nearby but never seemed to have much time for her.

Often, I would spend as much time in the house visiting as I did outside tending to the yard.

After graduating from high school, I lived at home for a few more years but eventually had to give up the gardening job since I was preoccupied with a new job and taking college classes. Later, I moved away and began a new life out of state.

On rare occasions when visiting my family, I would stop in to see her at the rest home where she had moved when she was no longer able to live alone. I introduced her to my fiancée, Lela, on one such visit, and she was thrilled with all that was going on in my life. She had heard I was getting married and gave us a wedding gift of a handmade crocheted pillow. That was the last time I saw her. That was over 30 years ago.

Recently while returning home from a family reunion, I rerouted the trip to pass through Allen. I drove my wife and two sons around town pointing to various important places from my past life in the little town. Before we got back on the highway that would lead us homeward, I wanted to see the little house that was once Sis Gardner's.

I had some doubts that I could find it quickly as I had not returned to the small town in many years. However, as I turned off Broadway, Allen's version of Main Street, I weaved through the residential area and easily found the road that lead to the more distant neighborhood where Sis Gardner's house sat. As I neared the intersection, I felt proud that I had remembered my way, as well as a quickening anticipation of seeing the place that held so many memories.

As we approached, I realized the house was gone. Instead, a weed-covered lot greeted us. There were no vivid pink and red azaleas or stunning white hydrangeas, no purple irises or orange and yellow lilies growing along the road. Even the Mimosa tree that once stood in the corner of the front yard was gone.

While I didn't expect it to be the same, since Sis Gardner had been gone for many years, I felt my breathing stop when I saw nothing but decay and neglect in place of what I once considered a beautiful and welcoming place.

Along with the impact of time and change came a sudden sadness, and I recalled a similar occurrence when I visited the property where I had spent so many summers and holidays visiting my grandparents. On that visit I had discovered a new house in place of the old one. The barn seemed much smaller and the lane where I had walked with cousins, brothers and sisters was shorter than I remembered. The sweet memories of my childhood had been tainted by the intrusion of my adult self who wanted to see it all again.

As we drove away from the empty lot at the corner of Camper Road and D Street, I looked back one more time to the empty, weed covered lot and half expected to at least see the old washtub lying in the spot that was once the side yard. Perhaps it was more of a longing than an expectation.

David Nickell is an adjunct professor of English Composition at Northwest Arkansas Community College in Bentonville, AR and at the University of Arkansas at Fort Smith, where he was recently awarded the Luella M. Krehbiel Adjunct Teaching Excellence Award. He also serves as Christian Education Director at Northside United Pentecostal Church in Fort Smith, AR. In his capacity as educator, both in the traditional classroom and in Christian ministry, David has taught every age group, from six to sixty. Growing up in "small town America" in southeastern Oklahoma, he has fond memories of get-togethers with extended family during the summer months and holidays. The influence of many strong role models in his life has created the strong to desire to keep faith, family and serving others as top priorities. David moved to the Arkansas River Valley in the early eighties. After marrying and beginning a family, he resumed his education as a non-traditional student. He holds a Bachelor of Arts in English from the University of Arkansas at Fort Smith and a Master's in English from Arkansas Tech University. When he isn't pouring over student essays or preparing for church events, David reads inspirational and biographical books. He is an avid John Grisham fan. For the past four years, he has been a member of the Singing Men of Arkansas, performing in a variety of venues across the region. As a fan of non-fiction writing, David's goal is to publish more of his own non-fiction work to inspire and entertain a Southern audience. He is currently working on a novel based on his father's experiences growing up in rural Oklahoma.

David currently lives in Van Buren with his wife, Lela, sons Reed and Alec and a rescue mutt, Rocco.

DARLING DAUGHTER

by Monieca West

Having children was never a priority for me. I would have been perfectly happy chasing a career instead. But after thirty-two years of being one, I can't imagine how empty a day would be without a call where the most familiar of voices says, "Mom, just a random thought but did you know…?"

Or a daughter that arranges for sixty notes from sixty of my friends to be given to me on my sixtieth birthday. Or one that now worries about me like I used to worry about her. These are the joys of motherhood that I am grateful I didn't miss.

This joy was not what was on my mind during the twenty-two hours of labor that produced Whitney Ann West. The joy didn't come during the first month when my biggest challenge was learning how not to kill my own kid.

Those first few weeks were such a blur of feeding, changing diapers and trying to get some sleep that I didn't have time to ponder perhaps the greatest experience a woman can have. She was a sweet little thing but I didn't really think of it as mothering so much as a project to be managed. However, there soon came a time when all doubts were rolled aside and I knew that I was a mother. For me, it was a family reunion when she was about two months old. Our family reunions were held in the camping area of the North Fork River in Saddle, Arkansas. It was an annual gathering of all of

Daddy's cousins and their offspring. This was back in the day when the generation before me still cooked routinely and their cooking was magnificent. Just thinking of the names—Betty, Novalene, Willa Faye, Laveda, Mary Faith—makes my mouth water. I couldn't wait to partake since I didn't produce that kind of home cooking.

July is hot in Arkansas, so hot that all Whitney did was sleep most of the day while I visited with everyone. As the day passed, I grew more excited about dinner when at last the older women laid it out. I was grateful Whitney was still sleeping because that meant I could really concentrate on fried chicken, potato salad, vegetables and oh my lord the desserts. I got in line, stacked my plate high and went back to my chair when Whitney started stirring and I had to tend to her. Of course, it was a nasty diaper and I did my best to clean her up on a pallet on the ground—without water to wash her or me, just the diaper wipes that I had with me. She was very good and went right back to sleep and I was very hungry and went right back to my plate.

I sat down, picked up my piece of corn on the cob and took a sweet bite. I happened to look down at my hands and saw this yellow stuff underneath my fingernails. Without missing a beat, I said "What the hell!" and kept right on eating. I figure that if you can eat corn on the cob with baby poop under your fingernails, you must be a mother! And so I was.

By the age of three, Whitney had grown into a beautiful and precocious little girl. I was no longer the mother of a dependent infant but a reasonable human being that could carry on a coherent conversation and accompany me without the fuss of diaper bags, bottles, stroller or toys.

DARLING DAUGHTER

Phil and I were fortunate to have very good jobs that allowed us to dress her like a princess and give her everything she could possible want. But, I admit there were times that I was flat broke. You know, the days right before payday when the bank account is empty and the only cash you have are the coins in the console of your car.

It was one of those weeks when Whitney wanted to go to McCain Mall to ride the train. I asked her if she would settle for the escalators, which were almost as much fun in her eyes as the train. She agreed and we set off for the mall with Whitney swinging her little red high-top tennis shoe purse over her shoulder.

When we arrived at the mall, she spotted the train and forgot all about the deal we made for the escalator option. I tried to explain that I didn't have enough money for the train ticket to which she promptly advised that SHE had "shoppin' cashes" and lo and behold she did. She unzipped her little tennis shoe purse and pulled out a crisp-fresh-from-the-bank $100 bill! Not being a fool, I quickly exchanged an assortment of pennies, nickels and dimes for the paper money and we were both very happy.

She rode the train several times and I bought lunch. Where her shoppin' cash came from is still not confirmed but we believe that she slipped into Phil's briefcase just before he left on a business trip after he had been to the bank for traveling money; or it could have been from his Oaklawn betting stash. Regardless, the little thief had helped herself to the cash and had been carrying her newfound funds around for who knows how long, while I had been rolling pennies to live on!

When I was a kid, two occurrences marked the arrival of spring— the Easter Bunny and cleaning up the yard. About this time of year,

Daddy would convene his kids in the front yard and we had to clean up the mess that had accumulated over the winter months. We had to pick up the bits and pieces of papers, limbs, stray cans and other matter that had either been tossed aside or blown in by the wind. So, when I became a parent and had a yard that got cluttered over the winter, I followed my dad's example and convened my only daughter Whitney in our backyard. She was going on four at the time and old enough to learn about chores and responsibilities.

It was a beautiful spring afternoon when I began explaining what we needed to do. It was clear from the outset that Whitney had no interest in gardening or landscaping or anything else related to manual labor. In fact, we stood toe-to-toe arguing about what she was going to do, why she was going to do it and her vehement refusal to go along with the plan.

I got the last word in, spun on my heel and started walking away. To this day, I don't know what made me stop and turn around to look at her. As I did, she bowed up with hands on hips and defiantly said, "What?"

I just stared at her for a split second trying to figure out what she was questioning when she said, "I wasn't spitting at you."

I lost my mind. She had spit at me when I turned my back on her. In the true fashion of my dad, I picked her up, tanned her little backside and plopped her down at the base of a tree. She was squalling, I was screaming and the neighbors were probably calling Child Services when my husband walked out onto the deck and asked, "What is going on here?"

I explained, "She spit at me… she stinking spit at me!"

He looked at Whitney who, in her best criminal defendant voice said, "I wasn't spitting at her, I was clearing my throat!"

To Phil's credit, he just smiled at her and suggested, "The next time you and your mom are arguing and you need to clear your throat you might want to tell her before you do it."

Whitney went inside and I finished cleaning up the yard just like I had for my dad those years ago. I learned: adult behaviors and attitudes are shaped by the behaviors learned from parents. Whitney learned that Moms truly have eyes in the backs of their heads! This served me well until she figured otherwise.

It's much easier being a good mom when there is an exceptional dad. Whitney was never confused about what the rules were even though she was not averse to working both sides of the table to get the answer she wanted. Phil and I shared a common parenting philosophy and had different but complimentary talents for parenting. I was always the one who took care of logistics and day-to-day maintenance. Phil was the developmental dad who taught her valuable life lessons such as how wise it is to never spit at your mother.

When Whitney was five, she made an appearance in the Ballet Arkansas production of The Nutcracker. The part was small but large enough in my mind to warrant a formal picture of her in her angel halo holding a nutcracker doll. As we were preparing for the photo session, Whit and I stood in front of the bathroom mirror while I pulled her hair up into the obligatory ballet bun. It was then that I noticed short shocks of hair sticking up along her forehead hairline. I knew immediately that she had cut her hair—an absolute no-no for ballerinas of any age.

As I began using my motherly "cleaning up the yard voice" to bring to her attention to what a dumb thing cutting her hair was, she began snubbing, trying not to cry. That did nothing to lower the volume of my voice and Phil came into the bathroom asking, "What is going on here?"

I proceeded to explain to him that his daughter had cut her hair and that ballerinas did not cut their hair. What was the darn picture going to look like now?

Being the good, developmental dad that he was, he turned to Whitney and said, "Whit, when you were looking into the mirror and about to cut your bangs, what did your stomach feel like?" Seeing a blank look on her face, he added, "You know, did it feel like there were butterflies in your stomach, flying around?" When she snubbed a quiet yes, Phil said, "Well, Whit. You should listen to your stomach. When it feels like butterflies, your stomach is telling you to think one more time about what you are about to do."

She was not old enough to conceptualize a guilty conscience but she could recognize the physical symptoms. Years later she says she still remembers the lesson of the butterflies and the other "pearls of wisdom" Phil shared with her.

Sometimes mothers learn more from a particular incident than the child does. I couldn't help but think that my life might have been easier had I listened to my stomach more often. As a teenager and young adult, Whitney made pretty good decisions and I've always given credit to Phil for her becoming a sensible and wise young woman.

DARLING DAUGHTER

Phil travelled a lot when Whitney was young but he rarely ever missed ball, dance or drama performances. As he was the baseball player in the family, I assumed that he would be the one to manage her T-ball career. But because of his travel, it fell to me to take her to her first game. It was a co-ed league with Whitney and one other little girl among the group of boys. The boys acted the way I expected them to, making it clear they didn't want girls playing. When Whit came to me crying, Phil wasn't there to impart his usual good advice so she had to settle for mine. I won't repeat my exact words but suffice it to say that I pulled no punches with her about being a woman in a man's world. I gathered her up onto my lap and told her the hard fact of life... little boys can be mean... and that she just had to go out there and be better than them.

Which she promptly did.

She could wallop the ball further than all but one little boy and it didn't take long for them to forget that she was only a girl. It was common for her to hit a double or triple but when she finally hit her first home run in the last game of the four-week season, the boys were her biggest cheerleaders. Her next at-bat found the bases loaded and she slugged one way out into left field (down third base line just like her dad). As she chugged around the bases, her smile grew wider, base by base. When she jumped onto home plate high-fiving with the boys, she turned to find me in the stands and said, "Mom, I hit a ham slam!" Phil and I were awfully proud of her then and proud now that she has never willingly taken a backseat to the boys.

I always thought that one of the best things that I could do for my daughter was to provide her with a role model of an accomplished professional. Whitney always saw me go to work in pearls, suit and heels while carrying a work satchel and my ever-present planner. One of my favorite suits was a black one that I wore with a gold silk blouse and an antique gold and black necklace.

Several years later I decided to sell off old things at a garage sale. When Whitney realized that I was selling clothes, she was aghast that I might have sold that particular suit. When I told her I had not, she was so relieved. She said, "You probably don't know this but when I was little, I would go into your closet after you left for work, put that suit on with some of your heels and I would boss the dogs!"

I guess if I bossed her, she was entitled to boss whoever was below her in the family hierarchy and that would have been Buddy and Murphy. I suppose she was practicing her future management style.

Our darling daughter has given her father and me amazing memories, family lore I never tire of remembering or telling. These stories tell the tale of her childhood and my motherhood. But the most wonderful realization that I have come to as a mother is that the journey didn't end with her youth. Just as I watched her discover childhood, navigate adolescence, and experience independence during college, I now watch her succeed professionally, guide and counsel her own child, and take care of a house and husband. She has grown into a beautiful, talented, thoughtful and wonderful young woman.

I may have started out ambivalent about having children but I now cannot imagine life otherwise. From the first poopy realization of motherhood, it is a role I have relished and am ever grateful to have experienced.

Monieca West is an economic and community development professional with both corporate and public sector experience. She currently manages a federal career and technical education program for the Arkansas Department of Higher Education. Her interests center on issues of poverty, career development, youth leadership and the advancement of women. She has received numerous awards for services to community organizations and public education in her hometown of North Little Rock, Arkansas, where she lives with her husband and two crazy cats. Writing, reading, quilting, and adventures with a new grandson are among her favorite ways to spend time.

WORD OF GOD IN MOTION
One Woman's Struggle To Save Her Family After Great Tradgedy

by Yolanda Winston

Chapter 1 Day of Reckoning

It was the day my estranged husband, Marcus, stood trial for the felony negligent homicide of our five-year-old son, Marquis. The prosecutors had delayed his trial for nearly three years, using excuse after excuse to keep my family and me suffering in our own private hell.

It was Marcus who was driving the car the day the accident took my precious little boy from this world and delivered him to God, September 23, 2011. Two to four months later, the Little Rock police arrested him based on blood tests from the hospital (the exact level wasn't revealed until the trial date). Not only was our family still grieving the loss of our beloved Marquis, but my two young daughters, Ashley and Aniya, were now facing the potential loss of their father as well.

The morning of the trial, I woke up very early with a huge knot in the pit of my stomach. Though pleased that the trial date had finally arrived, I was immensely anxious about having to sit in the courtroom and relive that horrific day all over again. I was terrified for Marcus and prayed repeatedly that God would spare him from incarceration. Not wanting to endure the traumatic day that lay ahead alone, I called my one friend (you know, the one we all have who will be there for you on a dime).

"Connetta," I begin with urgency in my voice. "Today is the day I have to go and listen to everything that happened to my Marquis and see all the pictures."

"Say no more," Connetta replied without hesitation. "Tell me where and when."

"I can meet you outside the Little Rock courthouse at nine," I answered, relieved that she would be able to accompany me during the trial. Before we hung up, Connetta said a prayer for my family and me.

On the two-and-a-half-hour drive from Fort Smith, Arkansas, where my daughters and I lived, to Little Rock, I tried hard not to let the tears that are streaming from my eyes prevent me from seeing the road. Those past three years had been one long and agonizing nightmare.

After members of my extended family found out about the car accident, they immediately turned on Marcus and wanted me to leave him. When I refused, they turned on me as well. The local newspaper ran an article the day after Marcus was arrested, which was very widely read.

From that day forward, my kids and I were treated like pariahs by the rest of my family, friends and community members because I didn't abandon Marcus right away. Not a single member of my extended family would agree to come to his trial with me; they all had come to revile Marcus and wanted him convicted, even if that meant my two daughters lost their father forever.

Though my eldest daughter Ashley had been angry with her father for the three years prior and their relationship was rocky, she wanted to go with me to his trial. Ashley wasn't very expressive of her feelings and mostly kept to herself, but she clearly didn't wish to see her father locked up.

I prayed a silent prayer: Dear God, , I beg you to have mercy on Marcus, and save him from jail. Please don't take him away from us forever.

Outside the Little Rock courthouse, an intimidating building within which so many have lost their lives to prison, I meet up with Marcus, Connetta, and Brenda (a powerful woman of God whom I asked to sit with me during the trial). Before going inside, we prayed together for a few moments and pleaded with God to deliver the best possible outcome.

As we entered the courtroom, I held my head up high knowing that all I had left was my complete faith in God. I did eventually separate from Marcus when his drug and alcohol addiction worsened in the months and years following the accident. I simply didn't have the strength to fight with him about it anymore. My full armor of God had been broken into little pieces and my breastplate was filled with bullet holes around my heart.

I finally had no alternative but to turn Marcus and his serious drug problems over to God, telling myself, that if God couldn't get his attention, then I sure wouldn't be able to.

Even though I eventually found the courage to separate from Marcus, I was still very concerned with his well-being and hated to see him waddle in drugs and alcohol as a way of coping with his immense guilt and shame over the accident. I realized, however, that if I didn't walk away he would take me down that self-destructive path with him, and I couldn't allow that to happen. I did remain his friend and biggest supporter and wanted nothing more than for him to get clean and sober and to become the man and father that I knew he could be.

Marcus, Connetta, Brenda, Ashley, and I took a seat on one of the long wooden benches near the front of the courtroom. Court was already in session and the judge was hearing a case about a man who intentionally caught his girlfriend on fire. That's some serious evil right there, I thought to myself.

Marcus's attorney saw him and waved him over. They disappeared into the hallway outside, presumably to discuss the details of his case. Moments later, a sharply dressed female prosecuting attorney introduced herself and requested to speak with me in the back of the courtroom. We were accompanied by one of her assistants. "Mrs. Winston," she began, "I am so sorry for your loss. How have you been doing?"

I immediately became suspicious of this woman's feigned concern for my well-being. "I'm doing fine," I responded tersely.

"There's nothing worse than losing your own child. I can't imagine how hard all this must be on you."

"Unless you've lost a child, you have no clue what it's like," I informed her directly.

She continued. "So, your husband was clearly under the influence at the time of the accident, and your five year-old-son, Marquis, was not wearing a seatbelt. This much is on the record. We are hoping that you will take the stand and testify today."

"Testify?" I reply with total surprise. "What would I have to testify about?"

"We'd like you testify about your husband's drug and alcohol problems."

I could tell from the look on their faces they were anxious to know if I'd agree to take the stand and help them convict Marcus. This unexpected request made me wonder whether their case against him wasn't as strong as they led me to believe. "I have no intention of testifying for ya'll," I told them defiantly.

Both women frowned in disappointment. "So, what is it that you want to happen here today?" The prosecuting attorney inquired. The softness that had been in her voice moments earlier was gone, replaced with a much sterner tone.

"What I want is for my family to be whole again. I want my family back," I told her. "Marcus has already paid the ultimate punishment for what happened. He must live with that for the rest of his life. I don't want him rotting away in a prison cell somewhere, how is that any good for my daughters?"

When I went back to my seat Connetta asked, "What did they want?"

"They wanted me to testify against Marcus."

"What did you tell them?"

"I told them to go to hell."

After a while, Marcus returned from his hallway meeting with his attorney. I could see from the grimace on his face that he was having a difficult time keeping himself together. I took his hand and whispered, "It's in God's hands now, and I really believe he will have favor on our family today."

Marcus's case could have been called at any time, so every time the current case concluded, we held our breath and waited anxiously to hear if he would be the next one called. There were some very serious crimes being adjudicated before the judge, and many of the defendants were being sentenced to prison. Though I didn't let it show, that made me worry about Marcus's fate even more than when we had first arrived. Hour after hour the courtroom became less full. Then around 4 pm, seven hours after we had first arrived, the judge called Marcus's case to trial.

Chapter Two: Marquis arrives from Heaven

I haven't always been a woman of God. In fact, when I became pregnant with Marquis in November of 2005, I was still very much a lost lamb in need of saving. My relationship with Marcus, the father of my two beautiful daughters, was very volatile at the time. He'd been out of prison for about a year when I found out we would be having a third child together.

Marcus was released in late 2004 and moved in with us at the newly built income-based apartment building, in North Little Rock, called Chapel Ridge. He was upset with me for not being faithful to him while he was locked up and it created a lot of friction between us.

Though we weren't married at the time, we were in a relationship and he fully expected me to wait for him. Because he had such difficulty forgiving me for my indiscretions, he was still bitter and would sometimes say things that were intended to bring me down or hurt my feelings. We would argue often and there were times when he would just disappear for days and I would have no idea where he was, what he was doing, or with whom. Other times, I would throw him out because he kept making it so hard for me to deal with his obnoxious and uncompromising behavior.

Though I was living in Section 8 housing, my income from my part-time job meant that I had to pay nearly the full rent, and this took up most of my weekly paychecks. To make ends meet, I started a side business doing women's hair. I had my barber's license but it didn't make any sense for me to pay a booth rental at some salon. Besides, I had two little daughters to take care of and styling hair was something I could do from home.

In addition to my part-time job and side business doing hair, I'd recently started a couple of classes at the local community college. I was a member of the National Guard and would go away one weekend a month for drills.

Whoever believes that everyone living in Section 8 housing is lazy and without dreams is entirely mistaken. There are plenty of impoverished people with dreams and the ambition to pursue them. Sadly, for many of them, the hardships of life keep getting in their way and beating them down until eventually they just give in to defeat. Not me.

Now that I had God in my heart I wasn't going to let anything, or anyone, deter me from making a better life for my children and me.

Yolanda Winston is an inspiration to women who have gone through a crisis in their lives, as well as to those who have proudly served our country. In her book, Word of God in Motion, Winston tells her compelling story about the tragic loss of her young son, how that loss affected her marriage and family, how she has struggled to heal and how she overcame tragedy to find happiness and success. Through Winston's story, you'll witness the extreme challenges she faced in her life and her deep faith in God, which carried her through. In January of 2000, Winston joined the Army National Guard. In 2006, Winston switched to the Air National Guard and became a Medical Records Clerk, serving with the 189th Airlift Wing. In 2013, she transferred to 188th Airlift Wing, where she was blessed to become a program manager for over 900 medical cases for the entire base. She has 16 years of faithful service.

Winston earned her Associate Degree in Health Services Management, Bachelor's Degree in Business Management, Master's Degree in Human Resource Development and is a published author.